POEMS FOR YOUNG CHILDREN

Compiled by Caroline Royds
Illustrated by Inga Moore

Doubleday & Company, Inc.
Garden City, New York

CONTENTS

Girls and Boys Come out to Play Anon. 5

Choosing Shoes Ffrida Wolfe 6

Where Go the Boats? Robert Louis Stevenson 7

Puppy and I A. A. Milne 8

Monday's Child Anon. 10

The Owl and the Pussy-Cat Edward Lear 12

The Hairy Toe Anon. 14

The Man who wasn't There Anon. 15

There was an Old Man with a Beard Edward Lear 16

There was a Crooked Man Anon. 16

Eletelephony Laura Richards 17

Fog Carl Sandburg 18

The Bat Theodore Roethke 19

The Four Friends A. A. Milne 20

The Tale of Custard the Dragon Ogden Nash 22

Steam Shovel Charles Malam 25

Calico Pie Edward Lear 26

Written in March William Wordsworth 28

Lavender's Blue Anon. 29

To Matthew

Copyright © 1986 by Kingfisher Books Limited.
First Edition in United States of America, 1986
First published in the United Kingdom under the
title READ ME A POEM
All rights reserved
Printed by South China Printing Company, Hong Kong

Library of Congress Cataloging-in-Publication Data
Main entry under title:

Poems for young children.

  Summary: An illustrated anthology of classic and
contemporary poetry by a variety of English and
American poets.
  1. Children's poetry, English. 2 Children's
poetry, American. [1. English poetry — Collections.
2. American poetry — Collections] I. Royds, Caroline.
II. Moore, Inga, ill.
PR1175.3.P58   1986   821'.008'09282   86-1290
ISBN 0-385-23524-0

In Just —   e. e. cummings   *30*
If all the World were Paper   Anon.   *31*
I Saw a Jolly Hunter   Charles Causley   *32*
From a Railway Carriage   Robert Louis Stevenson   *33*
You are Old, Father William   Lewis Carroll   *34*
The More It Snows   A. A. Milne   *36*
I had a Little Nut-Tree   Anon.   *37*
The Man in the Moon   Anon.   *38*
Fuzzy Wuzzy   Anon.   *39*
Today was not   Michael Rosen   *40*
The Tiger   William Blake   *42*
Cock Robin   Anon.   *44*
The Common Cormorant   Anon.   *46*
A Wise Old Owl   Anon.   *47*
The Tickle Rhyme   Ian Serraillier   *47*
Ducks' Ditty   Kenneth Grahame   *48*
Incey Wincey Spider   Anon.   *49*
A Frog he Would A-Wooing Go   Anon.   *50*
Some One   Walter De La Mare   *53*
Stopping by Woods on a Snowy Evening   Robert Frost   *54*
Silver   Walter De La Mare   *55*
from **The Bed Book**   Sylvia Plath   *56*
Twinkle, Twinkle, Little Star   Jane and Ann Taylor   *57*
Wynken, Blynken and Nod   Eugene Field   *58*
I See the Moon   Anon.   *60*
Matthew, Mark, Luke and John   Anon.   *61*

Girls and Boys Come out to Play

Girls and boys come out to play,
The moon doth shine as bright as day!
Leave your supper and leave your sleep,
Come with your playfellows into the street.
Come with a whistle, come with a call,
Come with a good will or come not at all.
Up the ladder and down the wall,
A halfpenny roll will serve us all.
You find milk and I'll find flour,
And we'll have a pudding in half an hour.

ANON.

Choosing Shoes

Ｎew shoes, new shoes,
Red and pink and blue shoes,
Tell me what would YOU choose
If they'd let us buy?

Buckle shoes, bow shoes,
Pretty pointy-toe shoes,
Strappy, cappy low shoes;
Let's have some to try.

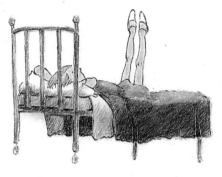

Bright shoes, white shoes,
Dandy dance-by-night shoes,
Perhaps-a-little-tight shoes;
Like some? So would I.

BUT
Flat shoes, fat shoes,
Stump-along-like-that-shoes,
Wipe-them-on-the-mat shoes
O that's the sort they'll buy.

FFRIDA WOLFE

Where Go the Boats?

Dark brown is the river,
　　Golden is the sand.
It flows along for ever,
　　With trees on either hand.

Green leaves a-floating,
　　Castles of the foam,
Boats of mine a-boating —
　　Where will all come home?

On goes the river
　　And out past the mill,
Away down the valley,
　　Away down the hill.

Away down the river,
　　A hundred miles or more,
Other little children
　　Shall bring my boats ashore.

ROBERT LOUIS STEVENSON

Puppy and I

I met a man as I went walking;
We got talking,
Man and I.
"Where are you going to, Man?" I said
(I said to the Man as he went by).
"Down to the village to get some bread.
Will you come with me?" "No, not I."

I met a Horse as I went walking;
We got talking,
Horse and I.
"Where are you going to, Horse, today?"
(I said to the Horse as he went by).
"Down to the village to get some hay.
Will you come with me?" "No, not I."

I met a Woman as I went walking;
We got talking,
Woman and I.
"Where are you going to, Woman, so early?"
(I said to the Woman as she went by).
"Down to the village to get some barley.
Will you come with me?" "No, not I."

I met some Rabbits as I went walking;
We got talking,
Rabbits and I.
"Where are you going in your brown fur coats?"
(I said to the Rabbits as they went by).
"Down to the village to get some oats.
Will you come with us?" "No, not I."

I met a Puppy as I went walking;
We got talking,
Puppy and I.
"Where are you going this nice fine day?"
(I said to the Puppy as he went by).
"Up in the hills to roll and play."
"I'll come with you, Puppy," said I.

A. A. MILNE

Monday's Child

Monday's child is fair of face,
Tuesday's child is full of grace,
Wednesday's child is full of woe,
Thursday's child has far to go,
Friday's child is loving and giving,
Saturday's child works hard for its living,
But the child that is born on the Sabbath day
Is bonny and blithe and good and gay.

ANON.

The Owl and the Pussy-Cat

The Owl and the Pussy-Cat went to sea
   In a beautiful pea-green boat:
They took some honey, and plenty of money
   Wrapped up in a five-pound note.
The Owl looked up to the stars above,
   And sang to a small guitar,
"O lovely Pussy, O Pussy, my love,
What a beautiful Pussy you are,
            You are,
            You are!
What a beautiful Pussy you are!"

Pussy said to the Owl, "You elegant fowl,
   How charmingly sweet you sing!
Oh! let us be married; too long we have tarried:
   But what shall we do for a ring?"
They sailed away, for a year and a day,
   To the land where the bong-tree grows;
And there in a wood a Piggy-wig stood,
   With a ring at the end of his nose,
            His nose,
            His nose,
With a ring at the end of his nose.

"Dear Pig, are you willing to sell for one shilling
        Your ring?" Said the Piggy, "I will."
So they took it away, and were married next day
        By the turkey who lives on the hill.
They dined on mince and slices of quince,
        Which they ate with a runcible spoon;
And hand in hand, on the edge of the sand,
        They danced by the light of the moon,
                        The moon,
                        The moon,
They danced by the light of the moon.

EDWARD LEAR

The Hairy Toe

Once there was a woman went out to pick beans,
and she found a Hairy Toe.
She took the Hairy Toe home with her,
and that night, when she went to bed,
the wind began to moan and groan.
Away off in the distance
she seemed to hear a voice crying,
"Where's my Hair-r-ry To-o-oe?
Who's got my Hair-r-ry To-o-oe?"

The woman scrooched down,
way down under the covers,
and about that time
the wind appeared to hit the house,

smoosh,

and the old house creaked and cracked
like something was trying to get in.
The voice had come nearer,
almost at the door now,
and it said,
"Where's my Hair-r-ry To-o-oe?
Who's got my Hair-r-ry To-o-oe?"

The woman scrooched further down
under the covers
and pulled them tight around her head.

The wind growled around the house
like some big animal
and r-r-um-mbled
over the chimbley.
All at once she heard the door cr-r-a-ack
and Something slipped in
and began to creep over the floor.

The floor went
cr-e-eak, cre-e-eak
at every step that thing took towards her bed.
The woman could almost feel
it bending over her bed.
Then in an awful voice it said:
"Where's my Hair-r-ry To-o-oe?
Who's got my Hair-r-ry To-o-oe?
You've got it!"

ANON.

The Man who wasn't There

As I was going up the stair
I met a man who wasn't there.
He wasn't there again today –
Oh, how I wish he'd go away.

ANON.

There was an Old Man with a Beard

There was an Old Man with a beard
Who said, "It is just as I feared! –
  Four Larks and a Wren,
  Two Owls and a Hen,
Have all built their nests in my beard!"

EDWARD LEAR

There was a Crooked Man

There was a crooked man, and he walked a crooked mile,
He found a crooked sixpence against a crooked stile;
He bought a crooked cat, which caught a crooked mouse,
And they all lived together in a little crooked house.

ANON.

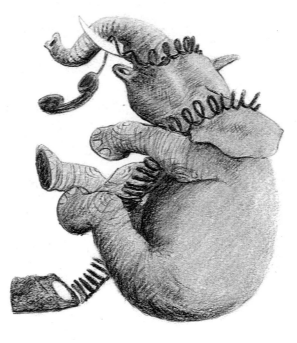

Eletelephony

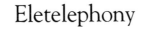

Once there was an elephant,
Who tried to use the telephant –
No! no! I mean an elephone
Who tried to use the telephone –
(Dear me! I am not certain quite
That even now I've got it right.)

Howe'er it was, he got his trunk
Entangled in the telephunk;
The more he tried to get it free,
The louder buzzed the telephee –
(I fear I'd better drop the song
Of elephop and telephong!)

LAURA RICHARDS

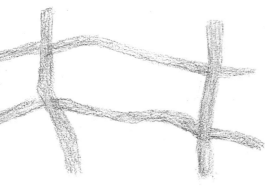

Fog

The fog comes
on little cat feet.
It sits looking

over harbor and city
on silent haunches
and then moves on.

CARL SANDBURG

The Bat

By day the bat is cousin to the mouse;
He likes the attic of an aging house.

His fingers make a hat about his head.
His pulse-beat is so slow we think him dead.

He loops in crazy figures half the night
Among the trees that face the corner light.

But when he brushes up against a screen,
We are afraid of what our eyes have seen:

For something is amiss or out of place
When mice with wings can wear a human face.

THEODORE ROETHKE

The Four Friends

Ernest was an elephant, a great big fellow,
  Leonard was a lion with a six-foot tail,
George was a goat, and his beard was yellow,
  And James was a very small snail.

Leonard had a stall, and a great big strong one,
  Ernest had a manger, and its walls were thick,
George found a pen, but I think it was the wrong one,
  And James sat down on a brick.

Ernest started trumpeting, and cracked his manger,
    Leonard started roaring, and shivered his stall,
James gave the huffle of a snail in danger
    And nobody heard him at all.

Ernest started trumpeting and raised such a rumpus,
    Leonard started roaring and trying to kick,
James went a journey with the goat's new compass
    And he reached the end of his brick.

Ernest was an elephant and very well-intentioned,
    Leonard was a lion with a brave new tail,
George was a goat, as I think I have mentioned,
    But James was only a snail.

A. A. MILNE

The Tale of Custard the Dragon

Belinda lived in a little white house,
With a little black kitten and a little gray mouse,
And a little yellow dog and a little red wagon,
And a realio, trulio, little pet dragon.

Now the name of the little black kitten was Ink,
And the little gray mouse, she called her Blink,
And the little yellow dog was sharp as Mustard,
But the dragon was a coward, and she called him Custard.

Custard the dragon had big sharp teeth,
And spikes on top of him and scales underneath,
Mouth like a fireplace, chimney for a nose,
And realio, trulio daggers on his toes.

Belinda was as brave as a barrelful of bears,
And Ink and Blink chased lions down the stairs,
Mustard was as brave as a tiger in a rage,
But Custard cried for a nice safe cage.

Belinda tickled him, she tickled him unmerciful,
Ink, Blink and Mustard, they rudely called him Percival,
They all sat laughing in the little red wagon
At the realio, trulio, cowardly dragon.

Belinda giggled till she shook the house,
And Blink said *Weeek!*, which is giggling for a mouse,
Ink and Mustard rudely asked his age,
When Custard cried for a nice safe cage.

Suddenly, suddenly they heard a nasty sound,
And Mustard growled, and they all looked around.
Meowch! cried Ink, and Ooh! cried Belinda,
For there was a pirate, climbing in the winda.

Pistol in his left hand, pistol in his right,
And he held in his teeth a cutlass bright;
His beard was black, one leg was wood.
It was clear that the pirate meant no good.

Belinda paled, and she cried Help! Help!
But Mustard fled with a terrified yelp,
Ink trickled down to the bottom of the household,
And little mouse Blink strategically mouseholed.

23

But up jumped Custard, snorting like an engine,
Clashed his tail like irons in a dungeon,
With a clatter and a clank and a jangling squirm
He went at the pirate like a robin at a worm.

The pirate gaped at Belinda's dragon,
And gulped some grog from his pocket flagon,
He fired two bullets, but they didn't hit,
And Custard gobbled him, every bit.

Belinda embraced him, Mustard licked him;
No one mourned for his pirate victim.
Ink and Blink in glee did gyrate
Around the dragon that ate the pyrate.

Belinda still lives in her little white house,
With her little black kitten and her little gray mouse,
And her little yellow dog and her little red wagon,
And her realio, trulio, little pet dragon.

Belinda is as brave as a barrelful of bears,
And Ink and Blink chase lions down the stairs,
Mustard is as brave as a tiger in a rage,
But Custard keeps crying for a nice safe cage.

OGDEN NASH

Steam Shovel

The dinosaurs are not all dead.
I saw one raise its iron head
To watch me walking down the road
Beyond our house today.
Its jaws were dripping with a load
Of earth and grass that it had cropped.
It must have heard me where I stopped,
Snorted white steam my way,
And stretched its long neck out to see,
And chewed, and grinned quite amiably.

CHARLES MALAM

25

Calico Pie

Calico Pie,
The little Birds fly
Down to the calico tree,
Their wings were blue,
And they sang "Tilly-loo!"
Till away they flew –
And they never came back to me!
They never came back!
They never came back!
They never came back to me!

Calico Jam,
The little Fish swam,
Over the syllabub sea,
He took off his hat,
To the Sole and the Sprat,
And the Willeby-wat –
But he never came back to me!
He never came back!
He never came back!
He never came back to me!

Calico Ban,
The little Mice ran,
To be ready in time for tea,
Flippity flup,
They drank it all up,
And danced in the cup –
But they never came back to me!
They never came back!
They never came back!
They never came back to me!

Calico Drum,
The Grasshoppers come,
The Butterfly, Beetle, and Bee,
Over the ground,
Around and round,
With a hop and a bound —
But they never came back!
They never came back!
They never came back!
They never came back to me!

EDWARD LEAR

Written in March

While Resting on the Bridge at the Foot of Brother's Water

The cock is crowing,
The stream is flowing,
The small birds twitter,
The lake doth glitter,
The green field sleeps in the sun;
The oldest and youngest
Are at work with the strongest;
The cattle are grazing,
Their heads never raising;
There are forty feeding like one!

Like an army defeated
The snow hath retreated,
And now doth fare ill
On the top of the bare hill;
The ploughboy is whooping – anon – anon:
There's joy in the mountains;
There's life in the fountains;
Small clouds are sailing,
Blue sky prevailing;
The rain is over and gone!

WILLIAM WORDSWORTH

Lavender's Blue

Lavender's blue, dilly, dilly,
　Lavender's green.
When I am king, dilly, dilly,
　You shall be queen.
Who told you so, dilly, dilly,
　Who told you so?
'Twas mine own heart, dilly, dilly,
　That told me so.

Call up your men, dilly, dilly,
　Set them to work,
Some with a rake, dilly, dilly,
　Some with a fork.
Some to make hay, dilly, dilly,
　Some to thresh corn,
Whilst you and I, dilly, dilly,
　Keep ourselves warm.

ANON.

In Just—

in Just—
spring   when the world is mud—
luscious the little
lame balloonman

whistles   far   and wee
and eddieandbill come
running from marbles and
piracies and it's
spring

when the world is puddle-wonderful

the queer
old balloonman whistles
far   and   wee
and bettyandisbel come dancing
from hop-scotch and jump-rope and

it's
spring
and
   the
      goat-footed
balloonman   whistles
far
and
wee

E. E. CUMMINGS

If all the World were Paper

If all the world were paper,
And all the sea were ink;
And all the trees were bread and cheese,
What should we do for drink?

ANON.

I Saw a Jolly Hunter

I saw a jolly hunter
   With a jolly gun
Walking in the country
   In the jolly sun.

In the jolly meadow
   Sat a jolly hare.
Saw the jolly hunter.
   Took jolly care.

Hunter jolly eager –
   Sight of jolly prey.
Forgot gun pointing
   Wrong jolly way.

Jolly hunter jolly head
   Over heels gone.
Jolly old safety-catch
   Not jolly on.

Bang went the jolly gun.
   Hunter jolly dead.
Jolly hare got clean away,
   Jolly good, I said.

CHARLES CAUSLEY

From a Railway Carriage

Faster than fairies, faster than witches,
Bridges and houses, hedges and ditches;
And charging along like troops in a battle,
All through the meadows the horses and cattle:
All of the sights of the hill and the plain
Fly as thick as driving rain;
And ever again, in the wink of an eye,
Painted stations whistle by.

Here is a child who clambers and scrambles,
All by himself and gathering brambles;
Here is a tramp who stands and gazes;
And there is the green for stringing the daisies!
Here is a cart run away in the road
Lumping along with man and load;
And here is a mill, and there is a river:
Each a glimpse and gone for ever!

ROBERT LOUIS STEVENSON

You are Old, Father William

"You are old, Father William,"
     the young man said,
   "And your hair has become
     very white;
And yet you incessantly stand
     on your head –
   Do you think, at your age,
     it is right?"

"In my youth," Father William
     replied to his son,
   "I feared it might injure
     the brain;
But, now that I'm perfectly sure
     I have none,
   Why, I do it again and again."

"You are old," said the youth,
     "as I mentioned before,
   And have grown most uncommonly fat;
Yet you turned a back-somersault
     in at the door –
   Pray, what is the reason of that?"

"In my youth," said the sage, as he
     shook his grey locks,
   "I kept all my limbs very supple
By the use of this ointment –
     one shilling a box –
   Allow me to sell you a couple?"

"You are old," said the youth,
     "and your jaws are too weak
   For anything tougher than suet;
Yet you finished the goose, with the
     bones and the beak –
   Pray, how did you manage to do it?"

"In my youth," said his father,
     "I took to the law,
   And argued each case with my wife;
And the muscular strength, which it
     gave to my jaw,
   Has lasted the rest of my life."

"You are old," said the youth,
     "one would hardly suppose
   That your eye was as steady as ever;
Yet you balanced an eel on the
     end of your nose –
   What made you so awfully clever?"

"I have answered three questions,
     and that is enough,"
   Said his father. "Don't give
     yourself airs!
Do you think I can listen
     all day to such stuff?
   Be off, or I'll kick you downstairs!"

LEWIS CARROLL

The More It Snows

The more it
SNOWS – tiddely-pom
The more it
GOES – tiddely-pom
The more it
GOES – tiddely-pom
On
Snowing.

And nobody
KNOWS – tiddely-pom
How cold my
TOES – tiddely-pom
How cold my
TOES – tiddely-pom
Are
Growing.

A. A. MILNE

I had a Little Nut-Tree

I had a little nut-tree,
  Nothing would it bear
But a silver nutmeg
  And a golden pear.

The King of Spain's daughter
  Came to visit me,
All for the sake
  Of my little nut-tree.

I skipped over ocean,
  I danced over sea;
And all the birds in the air
  Couldn't catch me!

ANON.

The Man in the Moon

The man in the moon
Came down too soon,
And asked his way to Norwich;
He went by the south
And burnt his mouth
With supping cold plum porridge.

ANON.

Fuzzy Wuzzy

Fuzzy Wuzzy was a bear;
Fuzzy Wuzzy had no hair.
So Fuzzy Wuzzy wasn't fuzzy. Was he?

ANON.

Today was not

Today was not
very warm
not very cold
not very dry
not very wet.

No one round here
went to the moon
or launched a ship
or danced in the street.

No one won a great race
or a big fight.

The crowds weren't out
the bands didn't play.

There were no flags no songs
no cakes no drums.
I didn't see any processions.
No one gave a speech.

Everyone thought today was ordinary,
busy busy
in out in
hum drummer day
dinner hurry
grind away day.

Nobody knows that today
was the most special day
that has ever ever been.

Ranzo, Reuben Ranzo,
who a week and a year ago was gone
lost
straying starving
under a bus? in the canal?
(the fireman didn't know)
was here, back,
sitting on the step
with his old tongue lolling,
his old eyes blinking.

I tell you –
I was so happy
So happy I tell you
I could have grown a tail –
and wagged it.

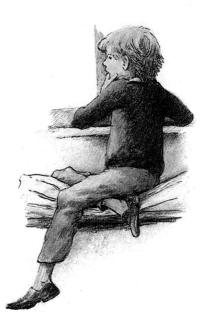

MICHAEL ROSEN

The Tiger

Tiger! Tiger! burning bright
In the forests of the night,
What immortal hand or eye
Could frame thy fearful symmetry?

In what distant deeps or skies
Burnt the fire of thine eyes?
On what wings dare he aspire?
What the hand dare seize the fire?

And what shoulder, and what art,
Could twist the sinews of thy heart?
And when thy heart began to beat,
What dread hand? and what dread feet?

What the hammer? what the chain?
In what furnace was thy brain?
What the anvil? what dread grasp
Dare its deadly terrors clasp?

When the stars threw down their spears
And watered heaven with their tears,
Did he smile his work to see?
Did he who made the Lamb make thee?

Tiger! Tiger! burning bright
In the forests of the night,
What immortal hand or eye
Dare frame thy fearful symmetry?

WILLIAM BLAKE

Cock Robin

Who killed Cock Robin?
I, said the Sparrow,
With my bow and arrow,
I killed Cock Robin.

Who saw him die?
I, said the Fly,
With my little eye,
I saw him die.

Who caught his blood?
I, said the Fish,
With my little dish,
I caught his blood.

Who'll make the shroud?
I, said the Beetle,
With my thread and needle
I'll make the shroud.

Who'll dig his grave?
I, said the Owl,
With my pick and shovel,
I'll dig his grave.

Who'll be the parson?
I, said the Rook,
With my little book,
I'll be the parson.

Who'll be the clerk?
I, said the Lark,
If it's not in the dark,
I'll be the clerk.

Who'll carry the link?
I, said the Linnet,
I'll fetch it in a minute,
I'll carry the link.

Who'll be chief mourner?
I, said the Dove,
I'll mourn for my love,
I'll be chief mourner.

Who'll carry the coffin?
I, said the Kite,
If it's not through the night,
I'll carry the coffin.

Who'll bear the pall?
We, said the Wren,
Both the cock and the hen,
We'll bear the pall.

Who'll sing a psalm?
I, said the Thrush,
As she sat on a bush,
I'll sing a psalm.

Who'll toll the bell?
I, said the Bull,
Because I can pull,
I'll toll the bell.

All the birds of the air
    Fell to sighing and sobbing
When they heard the bell toll
    For poor Cock Robin.

ANON.

The Common Cormorant

The common cormorant or shag
Lays eggs inside a paper bag
The reason you will see no doubt
It is to keep the lightning out.
But what these unobservant birds
Have never noticed is that herds
Of wandering bears may come with buns
And steal the bags to hold the crumbs.

ANON.

A Wise Old Owl

A wise old owl sat in an oak,
The more he heard, the less he spoke;
The less he spoke, the more he heard.
Why aren't we all like that wise old bird?

ANON.

The Tickle Rhyme

"Who's that tickling my back?" said the wall.
"Me," said a small
Caterpillar. "I'm learning
To crawl."

IAN SERRAILLIER

Ducks' Ditty

All along the backwater,
Through the rushes tall,
Ducks are a-dabbling,
Up tails all!

Ducks' tails, drakes' tails,
Yellow feet a-quiver,
Yellow bills all out of sight,
Busy in the river!

Slushy green undergrowth
Where the roach swim –
Here we keep our larder
Cool and full and dim.

Every one for what he likes!
We like to be
Heads down, tails up,
Dabbling free!

High in the blue above
Swifts whirl and call –
We are down a-dabbling,
Up tails all!

KENNETH GRAHAME

Incey Wincey Spider

Incey Wincey spider
  Climbing up the spout;
Down came the rain
  And washed the spider out:
Out came the sun
  And dried up all the rain;
Incey Wincey spider
  Climbing up again.

ANON.

A Frog he Would A-Wooing Go

A frog he would a-wooing go,
  Heigh ho! says Rowley,
A frog he would a-wooing go,
Whether his mother would let him or no.
  With a rowley, powley, gammon and spinach,
  Heigh ho! says Anthony Rowley.

So off he set with his opera hat,
  Heigh ho! says Rowley,
So off he set with his opera hat,
And on the road he met with a rat,
  With a rowley, powley, gammon and spinach,
  Heigh ho! says Anthony Rowley.

Pray, Mr.Rat, will you go with me?
  Heigh ho! says Rowley,
Pray, Mr.Rat, will you go with me,
Kind Mrs.Mousey for to see?
  With a rowley, powley, gammon and spinach,
  Heigh ho! says Anthony Rowley.

They came to the door of Mousey's hall,
  Heigh ho! says Rowley,
They gave a loud knock, and they gave a loud call.
  With a rowley, powley, gammon and spinach,
  Heigh ho! says Anthony Rowley.

Pray, Mrs.Mouse, are you within?
  Heigh ho! says Rowley,
Oh yes, kind sirs, I'm sitting to spin.
  With a rowley, powley, gammon and spinach,
  Heigh ho! says Anthony Rowley.

Pray, Mrs. Mouse, will you give us some beer?
    Heigh ho! says Rowley,
For Froggy and I are fond of good cheer.
    With a rowley, powley, gammon and spinach,
    Heigh ho! says Anthony Rowley.

Pray, Mr. Frog, will you give us a song?
    Heigh ho! says Rowley,
Let it be something that's not very long.
    With a rowley, powley, gammon and spinach,
    Heigh ho! says Anthony Rowley.

Indeed, Mrs. Mouse, replied Mr. Frog,
    Heigh ho! says Rowley,
A cold has made me as hoarse as a dog.
    With a rowley, powley, gammon and spinach,
    Heigh ho! says Anthony Rowley.

Since you have a cold, Mr. Frog, Mousey said,
    Heigh ho! says Rowley,
I'll sing you a song that I have just made.
    With a rowley, powley, gammon and spinach,
    Heigh ho! says Anthony Rowley.

This put Mr. Frog in a terrible fright,
   Heigh ho! says Rowley,
He took up his hat and he wished them good-night.
   With a rowley, powley, gammon and spinach,
   Heigh ho! says Anthony Rowley.

But as Froggy was crossing over a brook,
   Heigh ho! says Rowley,
A lily-white duck came and gobbled him up.
   With a rowley, powley, gammon and spinach,
   Heigh ho! says Anthony Rowley.

So there was an end of one, two, three,
   Heigh ho! says Rowley,
The rat, the mouse, and the little frog-ee.
   With a rowley, powley, gammon and spinach,
   Heigh ho! says Anthony Rowley.

ANON.

Some One

Some one came knocking
    At my wee, small door;
Some one came knocking,
    I'm sure – sure – sure;

I listened, I opened,
    I looked to left and right,
But nought there was a-stirring
    In the still dark night;

Only the busy beetle
    Tap-tapping in the wall,
Only from the forest
    The screech-owl's call,

Only the cricket whistling
    While the dewdrops fall,
So I know not who came knocking,
    At all, at all, at all.

WALTER DE LA MARE

Stopping by Woods on a Snowy Evening

Whose woods these are I think I know.
His house is in the village, though;
He will not see me stopping here
To watch his woods fill up with snow.

My little horse must think it queer
To stop without a farmhouse near
Between the woods and frozen lake
The darkest evening of the year.

He gives his harness bells a shake
To ask if there is some mistake.
The only other sound's the sweep
Of easy wind and downy flake.

The woods are lovely, dark, and deep,
But I have promises to keep,
And miles to go before I sleep,
And miles to go before I sleep.

ROBERT FROST

Silver

Slowly, silently, now the moon
Walks the night in her silver shoon;
This way, and that, she peers, and sees
Silver fruit upon silver trees;
One by one the casements catch
Her beams beneath the silvery thatch;
Couched in his kennel, like a log,
With paws of silver sleeps the dog;
From their shadowy cote the white breasts peep
Of doves in a silver-feathered sleep;
A harvest mouse goes scampering by,
With silver claws, and silver eye;
And moveless fish in the water gleam,
By silver reeds in a silver stream.

WALTER DE LA MARE

from The Bed Book

Most Beds are Beds
For sleeping or resting,
But the *best* Beds are much
More interesting!

Not just a white little
Tucked-in-tight little
Nighty-night little
Turn-out-the-light little
    Bed –

    Instead
A Bed for Fishing,
A Bed for Cats,
A Bed for a Troupe of
    Acrobats.

The *right* sort of Bed
(If you see what I mean)
Is a Bed that might
Be a Submarine

Nosing through water
Clear and green,
Silver and glittery
As a sardine

Or a Jet-Propelled Bed
For visiting Mars
With mosquito nets
For the shooting stars . . .

SYLVIA PLATH

56

Twinkle, Twinkle, Little Star

Twinkle, twinkle, little star,
How I wonder what you are!
Up above the world so high,
Like a diamond in the sky.

JANE AND ANN TAYLOR

Wynken, Blynken and Nod

Wynken, Blynken, and Nod one night
  Sailed off in a wooden shoe –
Sailed on a river of crystal light,
  Into a sea of dew.
"Where are you going and what do you wish?"
  The old moon asked the three.
"We have come to fish for the herring-fish
  That live in this beautiful sea;
Nets of silver and gold have we,"
  Said Wynken, Blynken, and Nod.

The old moon laughed and sang a song,
  As they rocked in the wooden shoe,
And the wind that sped them all night long
  Ruffled the waves of dew.
The little stars were the herring-fish
  That lived in that beautiful sea –
"Now cast your nets wherever you wish –
  But never afeared are we;"
So cried the stars to the fishermen three:
  Wynken, Blynken, and Nod.

All night long their nets they threw
  To the stars in the twinkling foam –
Then down from the skies came the wooden shoe,
  Bringing the fishermen home;
'Twas all so pretty a sail, it seemed
  As if it could not be,
And some folks thought 'twas a dream they'd dreamed
  Of sailing that beautiful sea –
But I shall name you the fishermen three:
  Wynken, Blynken, and Nod.

Wynken and Blynken are two little eyes,
 And Nod is a little head,
And the wooden shoe that sailed the skies
 Is a wee one's trundle-bed.
So shut your eyes while mother sings
 Of wonderful sights that be,
And you shall see the beautiful things
 As you rock on the misty sea,
Where the old shoe rocked the fishermen three:
 Wynken, Blynken, and Nod.

EUGENE FIELD

I See the Moon

I see the moon,
And the moon sees me.
God bless the moon,
And God bless me.

ANON.

Matthew, Mark, Luke and John

Matthew, Mark, Luke and John,
Bless the bed that I lay on;
Four corners to my bed,
Four angels round my head,
One to watch and one to pray,
And two to bear my soul away.

ANON.

Index of First Lines

A frog he would a-wooing go,   50
A wise old owl sat in an oak,   47
All along the backwater,   48
As I was going up the stair   15

Belinda lived in a little white house,   22
By day the bat is cousin to the mouse;   19

Calicoe Pie,   26

Dark brown is the river,   7

Ernest was an elephant, a great big fellow,   20

Faster than fairies, faster than witches,   33
Fuzzy Wuzzy was a bear;   39

Girls and boys come out to play,   5

I had a little nut-tree,   37
I met a man as I went walking;   8
I saw a jolly hunter   32
I see the moon,   60
If all the world were paper,   31
in Just –   30
Incey Wincey spider   49

Lavender's blue, dilly, dilly,   29

Matthew, Mark, Luke and John,   61
Monday's child is fair of face,   10
Most Beds are Beds   56

New shoes, new shoes,   6

Once there was a woman went out to pick beans,   14
Once there was an elephant,   17

Slowly, silently, now the moon   55
Some one came knocking   53

The cock is crowing,   28
The common cormorant or shag   46
The dinosaurs are not all dead.   25
The fog comes   18
The man in the moon   38
The more it   36

The Owl and The Pussy-cat went to sea   12
There was a crooked man,   16
There was an Old man with a beard   16
Tiger! Tiger! burning bright   42
Today was not   40
Twinkle, twinkle, little star,   57

Who killed Cock Robin?   43
"Who's that tickling my back?" said the wall.   47
Whose woods these are I think I know.   54
Wynken, Blynken, and Nod one night   58

'You are old, Father William,'   34

List of Poets

Blake, William   *42*

Carroll, Lewis   *34*

Causley, Charles   *32*

cummings, e. e.   *30*

De La Mare, Walter   *53, 55*

Field, Eugene   *58*

Frost, Robert   *54*

Grahame, Kenneth   *48*

Lear, Edward   *12, 16, 26*

Malam, Charles   *25*

Milne, A. A.   *8, 20, 36*

Nash, Ogden   *22*

Plath, Sylvia   *56*

Richards, Laura   *17*

Roethke, Theodore   *19*

Rosen, Michael   *40*

Sandburg, Carl   *18*

Serraillier, Ian   *47*

Stevenson, Robert Louis   *7, 33*

Taylor, Jane and Ann   *57*

Wolfe, Ffrida   *6*

Wordsworth, William   *28*

The editor and publishers gratefully acknowledge permission to reproduce the following copyright material:

Charles Causley: "I Saw a Jolly Hunter" from *Collected Poems*, Macmillan Publishers Ltd. Reprinted by permission of David Higham Associates Ltd. E. E. Cummings: "in Just" published in the UK in *The Complete Poems 1913-1962* by E. E. Cummings, Grafton Books (A Division of the Collins Publishing Group) and in the U.S.A. in *Tulips and Chimneys* by E. E. Cummings by permission of Liveright Publishing Corporation. Copyright 1923, 1925 and renewed 1951, 1953 by E. E. Cummings. Copyright © 1973, 1976 by The Trustees for the E. E. Cummings Trust. Copyright © 1973, 1976 by George James Firmage. Walter de la Mare: "Silver" and "Someone." Reprinted by permission of The Literary Trustees of Walter de la Mare and The Society of Authors as their representative. Eugene Field: "Wynken, Blynken and Nod" from *A Little Book of Western Verse* by Eugene Field published by Charles Scribner's Sons. Robert Frost: "Stopping by Woods on a Snowy Evening" published in the UK in *The Poetry of Robert Frost* and in the U.S.A. in *The Poetry of Robert Frost* edited by Edward Connery Lathem. Copyright 1923, © 1969 by Holt, Rinehart and Winston. Copyright 1951 by Robert Frost. Reprinted by permission of Holt, Rinehart and Winston, Publishers, Jonathan Cape Ltd. and the Estate of Robert Frost. Charles Malam: "Steam Shovel" from *Upper Pasture* by Charles Malam. Copyright 1930, © 1958 by Charles Malam. Reprinted by permission of Holt, Rinehart and Winston, Publishers. A. A. Milne: "The Four Friends" and "Puppy and I" from *When We Were Very Young* and "The More It Snows" from *The House at Pooh Corner*. Published in the UK by Methuen Children's Books and in the U.S.A. by E. P. Dutton. Copyright 1924 by E. P. Dutton, renewed 1952 by A. A. Milne. Reprinted by permission of the publisher, E. P. Dutton, a division of New American Library and Methuen Children's Books. Ogden Nash: "The Tale of Custard the Dragon" © Ogden Nash. Reprinted by permission of Curtis Brown Ltd., London and New York, Sylvia Plath: "from the Bed Book" from *The Bed Book* by Sylvia Plath, Faber & Faber Ltd., copyright Ted Hughes 1976. Reprinted by permission of Olwyn Hughes and Harper & Row Publishers Inc. Theodore Roethke: "The Bat" from *The Waking: Poems 1933-1953*. Reprinted by permission of Russell & Volkening, Inc. Michael Rosen: "Today" from *Wouldn't You Like to Know*. Reprinted by permission of Andre Deutsch Ltd. Carl Sandburg: "Fog" from *Chicago Poems* by Carl Sandburg, copyright 1916 by Holt, Rinehart and Winston, Inc.; renewed 1944 by Carl Sandburg. Reprinted by permission of Harcourt Brace Jovanovich Inc. Ian Serraillier: "The Tickle Rhyme" from *The Monster Horse* © 1950 Ian Serraillier and Oxford University Press. Reprinted by permission of the author. Ffrida Wolfe: "Choosing Shoes" from *The Very Thing*. Reprinted by permission of Sidgwick and Jackson.

While every effort has been made to obtain permission, there may still be cases in which we have failed to trace a copyright holder, and we would like to apologize for any apparent negligence.